· 10 ·
THINGS
Your Minister Wants
to Tell You

· 10 ·
THINGS
Your Minister Wants
to Tell You

+

*(But Can't, Because He
Needs the Job)*

+

Rev. Oliver *"Buzz"* Thomas

St. Martin's Press
New York

www.stmartins.com

Design by Kathryn Parise

LIBRARY OF CONGRESS CATALOGING-IN-PUBLICATION DATA

Thomas, Oliver S., 1955–
    10 things your minister wants to tell you : (but can't, because he needs the job) /
Oliver "Buzz" Thomas.—1st ed.
       p.   cm.
  ISBN-13: 978-0-312-36379-6
  ISBN-10: 0-312-36379-6
    1. Theology, Doctrinal—Popular works.   I. Title.   II. Title:
Ten things your minister wants to tell you.

BT77.T4545 2007
230—dc22

                           2006049680

First Edition: March 2007

10 9 8 7 6 5 4 3 2 1

To Professor Carlton Winbery,
who taught me that religion is something you do,
and the rest is just pious talk

Contents

✦

Contents

Acknowledgments

✦

Pat Summit, the great coach of the Tennessee Lady Vols, likes to say that too many people were born on third base and think they hit a triple. We all stand on somebody's shoulders. I stand on D.K. and Elma Lee Thomas's.

You'll understand something about my father if I tell you about how he died. He had a stroke that left his legs and arms paralyzed and his throat unable to swallow. After a few weeks, the doctor told Dad if he didn't let them put a feeding tube down his nose, he would die.

"Will it help me get well?" Dad asked.

"No, but it will keep you alive," his doctor replied.

"No, thanks," said my boyhood hero, and three days later he was dead.

If Dad taught me how to die, Mom taught me how to live. Flat out. She was still trick-or-treating in her seventies and holds the record for getting kicked out of the Wal-Mart parking lot when my brother was running for public office. One afternoon as she was passing out campaign literature, a man complained that she had already asked him to vote for her son. "That's all right," she said grinning, "we ask the good-looking ones two or three times!" If heaven has a bookstore, Mom will be there hawking this one for me.

I also want to pay tribute to my brother Kelly, my wife Lisa, and my daughters Rachel and Sarah. (Sarah, incidentally, is the real writer in the family.) Every old crow thinks her little crow is the blackest, but I don't know anyone with a more supportive family than mine. Without them, there wouldn't be 1 Thing, much less 10.

Then there are my mentors—The late Houston Goddard, Ray Frank Robbins, and Dean Kelley; the irrepressible James Dunn.

Finally, there are the faithful souls who helped me with this book. Reading early drafts, making suggestions, cheering me on. It's always risky to start a list because you're bound to leave someone out, but here goes: Herb Trammell (my father-in-law), Tom Garland, Brent Walker, Holly Hollman, Charles Haynes, David Saperstein, Roger Sullivan, John Burns, Linda Irwin, Kathy O'Dell, Nancy Dishner, Kay Dowdy, Maria and Brett Coulter, and Nancy and Jim Webber. A special thanks to Joe Hough, President of Union

Acknowledgments

Theological Seminary, without whom I would not have met my wonderful literary agent, Linda Loewenthal. And, then, there is my editor, Michael Flamini, whose intellect, humor, and grace keep me smiling while I work.

Finally, there are Scott and Nikki Niswonger and the board of directors of the Niswonger Foundation, who have provided me with an outlet for the expression of my faith. The ideas in this book are mine, not theirs, however, so any complaints or criticism should be directed solely at me.

Author's Note

✦

A word of explanation is due about how I intend to refer to the deity.

God is not a man. Nor is God a woman, for that matter, although the prophet Isaiah described God as such.

God is a spirit. A force. And, mostly, as the great Swiss theologian Karl Barth taught us, a *mystery*.

But God is also personal. At least the biblical writers thought so. So, the pronoun "it" doesn't seem to apply. In an attempt to make theology less inaccessible than it needs to be, I will also steer clear of the cumbersome he/she, opting instead for the more traditional singular masculine pronoun.

Admittedly, it's problematic. God probably has more characteristics we tend to associate with women (i.e., patient, nurturing, kind) than with men. Still, the traditional ways of referring to God can be useful when we are trying to introduce new ways of *thinking* about God. In short, I will probably lose fewer of you by sticking with the familiar "our father who art in heaven" than switching to "our mother." And, keeping you on board and interested is, after all, the point. Finding faith in the postmodern era is no easy task. We needn't make it more difficult than it has to be.

Preface

+

You can learn a lot about America by reading the *New York Times* bestseller list. What we like. What we don't. What challenges us or makes us laugh. It's a CAT scan of the nation.

One recent Sunday morning, I turned to the list and was jolted to find that two of the top three works of fiction were *religious*. Not that I dislike religion. I'm a minister, for Pete's sake.

It's that I had forgotten *we* were so religious. Not just the 40 percent who pack the pews each Sunday morning. *All* of us. Unlike our European counterparts, Americans *yearn* to connect with the eternal.

Despite MTV, Howard Stern, Paris Hilton, Monica Lewinsky, the Super Bowl halftime show, hip hop videos and all the rest, America remains a nation hungry for spiritual direction. We *want* to believe. (Just look at the number of people who still follow Jimmy Swaggart!) And we want our busy-beyond-measure lives to count for something.

But where is America's search for meaning leading her? What are we finding to feed our God-starved souls? Better yet, what would Jesus have to say about it if we could fast-forward him to the twenty-first century?

In the tradition of the great rabbis before him, Jesus made generous use of hyperbole. He wasn't above using a little exaggeration to drive home a point. Recall his frustrated retort to the prosperous fellow who refused to follow his sage advice about the dangers of money: "It's easier for a camel to pass through a needle's eye than for a rich man to get into heaven!"

Ouch.

Ask Jesus to describe America's spiritual diet, and he might just call it Kool-Aid. Worse yet, it may be Kool-Aid of the Jim Jones variety when it comes to our long-term spiritual health.

Let me explain.

The first of those two best sellers was an ode to sentimental spirituality—an appealing little fable about the five people you meet in heaven aimed straight at the heart. You learn some things you didn't know, work out the bad karma, and everyone lives happily ever after. No harm done, I suppose, but shouldn't healthy religion appeal to the head as well as the heart? And, what about the fact that it's all about *me*? Is that what authentic religion is really about?

The second best seller was the last of a series of fairy tales masquerading as "Biblical Christianity," which has made its authors the all-time best sellers of American fiction, surpassing even the prolific John Grisham. The stories include folks getting sucked out of cars, a genuine demon-possessed man ruling all the nations of the world, and Jesus of Nazareth coming back from heaven to unseat Satan and reign as a benevolent dictator for a thousand years with Jerusalem as his capital city. Great science fiction but based on a hop, skip, and jump use of biblical verses ripped out of their context and pasted together to form a farce that was rejected by the church and mainstream theologians a thousand years ago.

Once again, Kool-Aid.

Even today's popular prescription for a purpose-driven life flirts with the notion that the life of faith can be reduced to...well, a prescription. God in a box. It offers cocksure answers to some of life's most perplexing questions, all the while condoning the persistent ancient stereotypes of both women, who must be submissive—and gays, who must repent.

This book is written for all the people who want to live lives of purpose and meaning without having to put their brains in their pockets. It's written for the steeple dropouts who grew up on organized religion as well as for the millions of Americans who rise each Sunday to recite ancient creeds about virgin births and bodily resurrections, all the while feeling just a tad unconvinced.

A lot of this your ministers learned in seminary but were afraid to tell you from the pulpit for fear you would send them packing. With two kids and a mortgage, it was just too risky.

It's what ought to go on in Sunday school but usually doesn't. It's real. It's honest. It's relevant. And, most importantly, it's something you can live with.

The book is arranged around ten of life's most intriguing questions. And though grounded in the Hebrew and Christian scriptures, the answers are likely to surprise you. Much of this will be welcome ammunition to the 90 percent of Americans who have sat quietly while the firebrands of the far right have selectively quoted scripture as if it supported only one view—theirs. But, then, that's not surprising. All of us read scripture as if we were looking into a well. If we're not careful, we see only our reflections and miss the water entirely.

Jesus said we should love God with our minds as well as with our hearts. This book is going to help you do that.

Oliver Thomas
July 4, 2005

· 10 ·
THINGS
Your Minister Wants
to Tell You

· 1 ·

How Did It All Begin?

✦

I t all began with a police escort. Not the world, of course, but my understanding of just how important the question of origins had become to ordinary Americans. It was the spring of 1998, and the culture wars were heating up. In northern Alabama, they were sweltering.

My business partner and I had driven to the Dekalb County school district to provide *court-ordered* in-service training to about five hundred teachers on the subject of religion, including the teaching of creationism. Governor Fob James had declared war on the First Amendment, and we were caught in the cross fire. As I pulled to the curb, the police—and the protesters—were waiting for us.

"Wow," I remember saying, "we should have worn our flak jackets."

My partner smiled. "Yeah, it looks like there're more

protesters outside than teachers inside. Maybe we should just start the training out here."

We should have seen it coming. A year earlier and two thousand miles to the west, we had strolled into a California gymnasium packed for a school board meeting on the same set of topics. The town had become so divided that the pro-creationism people sat on one side and the anticreationism people on the other. Writing school policy was becoming a blood sport.

Today the battle has spread to virtually all fifty states, and despite the court's unequivocal decision to stymie a pro-creationist school board in Dover County, Pennsylvania, other cases are still pending. But before we get bogged down in the latest court decision, let's take a step back and examine what our religious traditions actually teach us about the origin of life.

The Christian and Hebrew scriptures begin with a bang. Not the big one of twentieth-century notoriety, but a bang nonetheless. It's a double bang, really, since the book of Genesis contains not one but *two* separate creation stories.

Bet you didn't know that.

The first and more familiar story is contained in Genesis 1 and begins with these simple yet elegant words: "In the beginning God created the heavens and the earth." The writer, most likely a priest, then proceeds with one of literature's most familiar stories. It is cast in the form of a poem and may even have been sung in the early Hebrew community. And, like most poems, it was never intended to be taken literally.

Come to think of it, no one should be entrusted to interpret Scripture who doesn't have a poet living inside him. Jesus sure did. How else could you talk about camels passing through the eye of a needle or God's concern over the lost sheep of Israel? Those surely weren't literal sheep. So, why, then, must it be a literal twenty-four-hour day?

The truth is that the word your Bible translates as *day* doesn't always mean a twenty-four-hour time period in Hebrew. It is also used to describe time periods of undesignated duration. Epochs, even. There's nothing to say that God couldn't have put natural forces into effect that took millions of years to reach fruition.

Then, there's the name given to the man in the story. *Adam* is the Hebrew word for all of mankind, not an individual's name like Abraham or Ezekiel. If we're supposed to be taking this story literally, why didn't the writer give us a real name?

If you're still not convinced, there are even more obvious cues that this is not to be taken literally. Light is created before the sun, moon, and stars. Think about that for a minute. The earth is *flat* with waters under it and over it. The waters over it are held out by a clear dome or "firmament." (To a prescientific mind, what else could account for the sky's blue color if not water?) Later, in the book of Malachi, we learn that this firmament has windows in it that God opens from time to time to let down the rain. (There must be water up there for it to rain!) The first creation story culminates with the creation of mankind, whom God creates "in his own image" ("Male and Female created he them.")

The second creation story begins in Genesis 2:4. (Remember, the chapter and verse designations were added centuries later.) This writer lacks the poetic flair of his priestly counterpart. He shortens things and switches around the order but in the end gives us a new story that men couldn't resist, so it gets grafted onto the first creation story as if it were part of the original. It is the story of woman being created from the rib of man and her subsequent role in introducing sin into the idyllic world God created. She does this by enticing the man to eat the forbidden fruit from the tree of knowledge. Handy stuff for a patriarchal society bent on keeping women in their place. It's worked so well, in fact, that as recently as the 1980s, a Southern Baptist Convention resolution justified the denomination's shabby treatment of women by referring to their being second in creation yet "first to sin."

Both creation stories, though different in the detail, tell us two important things about how life came to be. First,

God did it. We are not here by accident. There is a mysterious, creative force in the universe we call "God," and all of creation—including man—stand under his dominion. Second, life is good. And if anything seems screwed up, it's our fault, not his. (Note to self: The next time tragedy strikes, don't ask why God allowed this. God *allows* everything. It doesn't mean he approves.)

Some readers may be surprised to learn that these stories in the book of Genesis are not unique to ancient literature or to Judaism and Christianity. Several creation stories actually predate the Genesis accounts. In one of my favorites, a dragon literally vomits the world into existence. The great Hebrew prophet Isaiah, speaking centuries later, refers to the dragon in a passing slap, saying simply that the Hebrew God "cut him to pieces."

If the creation stories of Genesis are not intended as literal scientific accounts, how do we use our twenty-first-century knowledge to make sense of what God is trying to tell us here? More specifically, how do Darwin, the big bang, and punctuated equilibrium fit into a worldview that says we are not here by accident?

First, to the extent it helps us understand how life came to be, scientific study should be encouraged, not feared. Healthy religion seeks the truth. Certainly Jesus encouraged truth seeking when he told his disciples, "You shall know the truth, and the truth shall make you free!" Rabbis across the ages have done likewise. The great Jewish scholar Maimonides put it like this, "One should accept the truth from whatever source it proceeds."

Think about what Jesus and Maimonides are saying. Perhaps religion and science have nothing to fear from each other. At least if they are true to themselves.

Science and religion operate in different domains. Religion deals with what theologian Paul Tillich called "ultimate concerns"—abstract philosophical questions such as what the nature of life is and why we are here. Religion seeks meaning, purpose, and moral truth, not physical knowledge.

Science, on the other hand, seeks to understand the natural, observable world around us. Unlike religion or philosophy, the claims of science are falsifiable. That is to say, they are capable of being proven or disproven. Scientific progress is only made as its hypotheses are rigorously tested, analyzed, and refined.

While science asks us to accept nothing on faith, religion asks little else. No one can prove whether there is one God or many gods or whether God's spirit is alive in a particular human being, but we can most certainly prove whether the earth is six thousand years old or six billion years old. In short, science is an essential tool to understanding the world in which we live. Science cannot, however, tell us *how* to live or answer our ultimate questions.

As dominant as science has become in our world, we might be tempted simply to discount *anything* that is impervious to its probing finger, including religion, but that would be a mistake. The truth is that the things we care about most deeply—starting with love—lie beyond the reach of science.

Consider again the question of origins. If, for example, scientists are able to take us back to a big bang, nagging questions remain. Why did it all happen in the first place? For what purpose? What does it all mean? How should we then live? Only the philosophers and theologians can help us here.

Occasionally scientists venture outside their discipline and into the realm of theology. Carl Sagan was guilty of this when he opined that the cosmos "is all there was, is, or ever will be."

Says who? Or, better yet, prove it!

When scientists give in to the temptation to address ultimate concerns, the result is "scientism"—philosophy masquerading as science. Sagan's statement is no more scientific than that of the fundamentalist preacher who claims that God created the universe in six twenty-four-hour days.

Similarly, religion can masquerade as science. Consider the Christians who ask public schools to give "balanced treatment" to creationism and evolution. Creationism is not an alternative scientific theory. It is a nonfalsifiable claim that a divine being intervened in the natural order to create life. Calling a cow a billy goat doesn't make it one, and calling creationism "intelligent design" doesn't make it any less religious. It's still a nonfalsifiable claim that a super-natural force (which by definition is one coming from *out-side* the natural order) accounts for life on earth. Intelligent design is just creationism in a suit.

Forcing science teachers to teach a particular theological view is like a judge instructing a witness to testify that the light was red whether the evidence supports it or not. Science teachers must be free to teach their discipline without the constraints imposed by one religious view or another. Hard, factual truth is the objective, not precon-ceived notions about how life came to be.

So, is there any common ground when it comes to what should be taught in the nation's public schools? Yes. The an-swer seems to lie in simply teaching about the controversy. Tell kids the truth! Students should be taught the predomi-nant scientific view, no doubt, but they should also be alerted to the fact that not everyone agrees. Not even all sci-entists agree! A small minority of scientists consider the ev-idence for evolution to be spotty and unpersuasive. We shouldn't give them equal time, but a liberal education de-mands that students be alerted to their views and to the on-going debate about how life began.

When science and religion stick to their respective realms, all of society benefits. Science helps us understand the world around us, and religion helps us make sense of it all.

In this case, good fences really do make good neighbors.

· 2 ·

Why Are We Here?

✦

W ho am I and why am I here?" Admiral James Stock-
dale's bewildered comment during the 1992 vice
presidential debate is remembered as one of the funniest,
and most human, moments in American political history.
But his not-ready-for-prime-time remark is really the question for the ages. Why *are* we here? And now that we're
here, what is it we're supposed to be doing?

Poets and philosophers through the ages have answered
the question in a million ways, but Christianity's answer
has been nearly singular. We are here to glorify God.

Every time I hear it, I cringe. "Is that it?" I want to ask. Or,
as Peggy Lee famously put it, "Is that all there is?"

Worshiping and praising God has its place. An important one, no doubt. Most Americans try to worship at least

once a week, and we pray more than that. But life is more than worship and praise. As the writer of Ecclesiastes put it, "For everything there is a season. And a time for every purpose under heaven."

In addition to glorifying God, we are here to eat, drink, dream, dance, work, play, fish, make love, comfort, cry, celebrate, and a thousand other things. We are, in short, here to be *human*. Made in the image of God but different from God. Very different.

God, for example, has the luxury of silence. We don't. We must talk if we are to communicate with each other, and our talking gets us into trouble.

God has no physical body. No penis or vagina. No estrogen or testosterone. I won't even start on the troubles those can cause. God has never been to the emergency room, much less the coronary care unit. God has never taken a milligram of Prozac. As best we know, God will never have to die. God is, after all, God. But, he has made *us* human, and human we shall surely be.

So, what does it mean to be fully human?

The Hebrew scriptures, with their characteristic frankness, tackle the question head-on, eschewing some of the more pious answers traditionally associated with religion. The writer of Ecclesiastes (whom many believe to have been King Solomon) gives four concise directives: (1) eat, drink, and be merry; (2) work hard; (3) enjoy living with the person you love; and (4) fear God and keep his commandments. Simple, sensible and hard to argue with.

The New Testament also offers some clues. Consider Jesus' great summation of the good life found in Matthew 22 and Luke 10.

First, he said we should love God. Now, loving God is a challenge. For starters, he's a spirit. An abstraction. We can't rush into his arms and give him a hug. We can't send him a birthday present. He has no e-mail address. But we must be able to love him, otherwise our greatest souls—from Moses to Mother Teresa—wouldn't have instructed us to try. So, how do we do it?

We've already mentioned worship and praise. Surely that's one way to love God. For me, singing the great hymns of the church is one of my favorite ways to express my love and devotion to God. For others, there are the sacraments.

Prayer is yet another way to love God. Lots has been written about this fascinating subject, but boiled down to its essence, prayer is nothing more than conversation with God—talking and listening but not necessarily asking.

But what about the asking? Does it work? Multitudes attest that it does. Although the most comprehensive study of prayer to date suggests no connection between prayer and physical healing, those doing the praying in that particular study were strangers to the people for whom they were praying. When the prayers are offered on behalf of oneself or a loved one, they oftentimes work. We may argue about why they work, but work they do. At least in some cases.

Researchers at the University of Mississippi Medical Center, for example, recently presented a study of more than five thousand African Americans to the American Society of Hypertension, which showed (to the researchers' great surprise) that those who prayed and worshiped regularly had lower blood pressure readings than those who didn't, even when they forgot to take their medication! Whether it's the result of divine intervention or the simple relaxation that occurs when individuals engage in prayer and meditation is hard to say. What isn't hard to say is that for many people, prayer works.

One question pertaining to prayer has always intrigued me. If God is all-loving and all-knowing, as most Jews and Christians believe, why should we pray for anybody? Doesn't God know about their problems before we do? And, better still, what sort of God would he be if we sinful humans had to talk him into helping anybody? Doesn't he want them to get well more than we do?

Before you jump on my bandwagon, let me share with you a curious story Jesus once told about the importance of prayer. It's recorded in Luke 18:2–8:

In a certain city there was a judge who neither feared God nor regarded man; and there was a widow in that city who kept coming to him and saying, "Vindicate me against my adversary." For a while he refused; but afterward he said to himself, "Though I neither fear God nor regard man, yet because this widow bothers me, I will vindicate her, or she will wear me out by her continual coming." And the Lord said, "Hear what the unrighteous judge says. And, will not God vindicate his elect who cry to him day and night? Will he delay long over them? I tell you he will vindicate them speedily."

How's that for an interesting portrayal of our heavenly father?

I can reconcile the story with the notion of a loving God only by reminding myself that parables are not allegories and have only one point, which in this case is that persistence pays. But *why* does it pay? Does it pay because God is ornery, and he needs us to change his mind? I don't think so. The entire Judeo-Christian tradition hinges on the belief that God's attitude toward humanity is one of benevolence. If "God is love," as the Bible teaches, we certainly don't need to change his mind.

If not his attitude, then, what about his actions? Perhaps God has deliberately chosen to intervene in earthly affairs as infrequently as possible. Suppose he has put in place a universe governed by natural laws that should not be disturbed. Jesus seems to be saying that sometimes God is willing to intervene. When or why we're not entirely sure, but that he does seems a distinct possibility. That's one possible explanation for the many healings and other mysterious phenomena for which science seems unable to account.

The most constant, most reliable, most certain effect of prayer, however, is not on God. It's on us. Prayer transforms *us*. It gets us out of our self-oriented way of thinking and into God's way of thinking. It takes the spotlight off us and puts it on others. The great prayer of Saint Francis says it best:

Lord, make me an instrument of your peace. Where there is hatred, let me sow love; where there is injury, pardon; where there is doubt, faith; where there is despair, hope; where there is darkness, light; where there is sadness, joy. Oh, Heavenly Father, grant that I may not so much seek to be consoled as to console, to be understood as to understand, to be loved as to love. For it is in giving that we receive; it is in pardoning that we are pardoned; it is in dying (to self) that we are born to eternal life.

So, we pray not so much so He can hear us, but so we can hear him. Prayer is a slow but steady way of bending our will toward God's will. Pray long enough about someone else's problems, and you're likely to wind up helping him solve them.

The final and most important way that we love God, though, isn't through prayer or praise, as important as these may be. It is by loving other people. Especially those to whom Jesus referred as "the least of these"—the homeless alcoholic, convicted felon, battered wife, hungry child, or AIDS victim. "Love these," said Jesus, "and you have loved me."

Lots of ministers might stop right here but not if we're to be fully human. If we are to love our neighbors "as ourselves," first we must love ourselves.

So, love yourself!

I don't mean for us to overindulge, and I certainly don't mean to disguise our unhealthy greed, materialism, or self-absorption as healthy self-love. Loving ourselves, like loving our children, means seeking what's good for us. Not just what pleases us. Healthy self-love is a balance of self-discipline and self-indulgence. For example, I should take a vacation, but probably not one that costs $10,000. I should have a piece of fudge but probably not the whole pan. I need a new car but maybe not a Jaguar. You get the picture.

Loving oneself is an essential part of being a healthy human. Orienting our lives and priorities around ourselves, on the other hand, is the essence of what the Bible calls sin. Like much of life, it's a balancing act.

Why are we here? To be fully human.

What does it mean to be fully human? Loving and being loved.

If we can manage that, I suspect God will have had all the glory he wants.

· 3 ·

What Is the Bible?

The story is told that when the great humanist scholar Erasmus was commissioned to create a new, more reliable translation of the Bible in the sixteenth century, he wound up in a pickle. It seems that the church wanted to change the wording of the First Letter of John to be more in line with its doctrine of the Trinity. Church leaders hadn't given voice to the doctrine until two centuries after the death of Christ, due in no small measure to the fact that the Trinity is never mentioned in the books of the New Testament. Here was a chance to change all that. All Erasmus had to do was change the passage about the three witnesses—"water, blood, and the spirit"—to read "Father, Word [John's term for "Son"], and Holy Ghost," and the church's problem would be solved. The hitch was that *none* of the dozen or so Greek manuscripts available at that time (or since) supported this change. "Just bring me *one* such manuscript," thundered the great scholar, "and I'll make the change!"

So they did.

We shouldn't be too surprised, I suppose. The temptation to make a book say what you want it to say is just too great when you're the one controlling the process. It reminds me of what my old Irish Catholic uncle used to say: "Trying to use the Bible to prove the church wrong is like trying to use the phone book to prove there isn't a phone company."

So what do we need to know about this book that stands at the heart of our faith tradition? After all, no Bible? Then no Judaism or Christianity.

In truth, the Bible is a collection of books—some short, some long. None in English. And, despite popular belief to the contrary, they are not in the chronological order and do not lend themselves to being read straight through, despite what your grandfather may have told you.

In the Hebrew Bible, or Old Testament as Christians call it, there is the law (including the Ten Commandments, the story of the patriarchs, the Exodus, and the conquest of Palestine), the prophets (the great preachers of their day), and the writings (including the Psalms and a cache of pithy sayings known as the wisdom literature). All told, there are thirty-nine books in the Hebrew Bible. The process of selecting these books went on for more than seven hundred years, with the final list coming as a defensive measure only after dozens of Christian books began circulating in first-century synagogues.

A similar process happened with the New Testament. In the days following Jesus' crucifixion, his disciples simply passed along their stories by word of mouth. As far as we know, Jesus never wrote anything, and his disciples generally followed suit. They were unlettered peasants by and large, so their preference for the spoken word is not surprising. Most likely, many were illiterate.

It was some twenty years after Jesus' death when the Apostle Paul began writing letters of instruction to the churches he had helped start. These letters began circulating among the small bands of believers, sometimes as a single letter, sometimes as a collection of letters. Fifteen years later, Mark wrote the first account of Jesus' life and ministry. One early church father cites Simon Peter, one of Jesus' inner circle, as Mark's primary source. By then, Peter was under arrest in Rome awaiting execution. Matthew and Luke followed shortly with books of their own, and John's gospel was added near the close of the century, most likely by some of his former students.

Aside from the disciples' humble origins, there were more compelling reasons for the delay in recording the teachings of Jesus. First, writing books in the ancient world was an expensive and time-consuming process. There was also no effective means of copying and distributing books once they were written. Because early church leaders expected Jesus to return to earth during their lifetimes, time was too precious to spend writing one tedious manuscript at a time. In the short run, it was far more effective to preach to as many people as you could as often as you could. Only after Jesus failed to return as expected and eyewitnesses to his ministry began dying off did church leaders begin writing things down.

As with the Hebrew scriptures, the New Testament first began circulating in the churches as individual books. It would be several hundred years before the church decided on the official list of twenty-seven. Even today, Roman Catholics and Orthodox Christians continue to view certain books that are ignored by Protestants to be authoritative. To top it off, these two ancient halves of the Catholic tradition don't even agree on which books these are!

So what are we to make of this book that motivated such icons as Albert Schweitzer and Mother Teresa while at the same time inspiring some of history's bloodiest conflicts? After all, even the relatively minor nineteenth-century American squabble over which version of the Bible would be read in the public schools (the Protestant King James or the Catholic Douay) led to convents being burned and rioting in the streets of such cities as Boston, Philadelphia, and

Cincinnati. Some actually died in these so-called Bible Wars. More recently, the nation's largest Protestant group, the Southern Baptist Convention, engaged in a decades-long conflict over which words should be used to *describe* the Bible. Is it inerrant, infallible, or merely authoritative? Hundreds of ministers and scores of professors in church-related schools lost their jobs as a result.

Is the Bible literally the word of God, as fundamentalists claim, or is it better understood as a human, and therefore fallible, witness to the relationship between God and humans that has evolved over the centuries?

First, let's consider the claim that the Bible is the inerrant (i.e., without error) word of God.

As an introductory matter, many Americans are nonplussed that anyone living after Kepler, Copernicus, and Galileo (all who disproved the biblical view that the earth is the center of the universe) and Christopher Columbus (who certainly disproved the biblical view that the earth is flat) could cling to the comforting notion of an "inerrant" Bible. Yet the fact that nearly twenty million Baptists say they do necessitates that we at least consider the possibility.

Let us begin by saying that subjecting this fundamentalist claim to scrutiny is by no means a slap at the Bible. On the contrary, the Bible is the single most important book in history and is considered authoritative by nearly half the planet, including most Christians, Muslims, and Jews.

However, the persistent belief that a book that condones both slavery and the exploitation of women floated down from heaven precisely as it was dictated by God must be confronted if churches and synagogues are to have real moral authority in the twenty-first century.

We'll start with a simple question that must be answered by anyone who claims the Bible is inerrant. Which manuscript are they talking about? There are more than five thousand Greek manuscripts of the New Testament alone, yet no two are alike! If one is going to claim that a text is inerrant, he should at least be forced to identify the text to which he is referring. The pat answer so often given is the "originals"—meaning the manuscripts actually penned by the authors. Since these were lost or destroyed ages ago, it's an easy cop-out to the real and troubling questions that exist about the text that we do have. Instead of wasting time arguing about a biblical text that exists only in theory, we will confine our discussion to the text that actually exists.

Let's turn first to the painfully obvious biblical errors. The only way around these is for people simply to pretend they don't exist. Again, this first group of biblical inconsistencies are not errors of theology or ethics. They are simply logical or mathematical impossibilities. A few examples will suffice, but there are dozens.

1 Kings 7:23 purports to give the formula for the circum-

ference of a circle. In doing so, it values pi at 3 instead of 3.14 as we now know it to be. Close, but by no means inerrant.

Genesis and the Acts of the Apostles give inconsistent accounts of Abraham's departure from his home in present-day Iraq. One has him leaving before his father's death, the other after.

Matthew, Mark, and Luke list the date of Jesus' crucifixion as being the day after Passover. John has it occurring twenty-four hours earlier. Even the resurrection accounts are hopelessly inconsistent. Each of the four gospel writers has a different cast of characters announcing the event to the first arrivals at Jesus' garden tomb. Depending on whom you read, the news is announced by a young man, an angel, two young men, or two angels.

The best explanation for such biblical inconsistencies is the simple fact that they didn't matter. The gospel writers were trying to convey what they considered to be an earth-shaking religious event. Whether there were one, two, or twenty people present to announce it was irrelevant. The point was that it happened.

Other biblical errors are best explained through the use of historical research and interpretation. One of my favorites is found at 2 Samuel 24:1 and its companion passage at 1 Chronicles 21:1. At issue is the census taken during the reign of King David to count both the number of Israelites, as well as their horses, chariots, and other tools of war. The

Hebrew prophets had warned against such a census, claiming it might lead the Israelis to become a proud and boastful people who trusted in themselves rather than the God who had delivered them from bondage in Egypt.

Not surprisingly, the chronicler, having heard these prophetic pronouncements, attributes the inspiration for the census to Satan. Readers of the passage in Kings, however, are shocked to find the same census attributed to *God*. The explanation, though simple, is lost to the average reader.

Hebrew theology—like all theology—has evolved. Chronicles was written after dualistic notions (largely from Persia) of good and evil or God and Satan had made their way into Hebrew ways of thinking. Kings, on the other hand, was written centuries earlier when the Hebrew people were so radically monotheistic that all things— whether good or evil—were attributed to God. If your children prospered or they died prematurely, God did it—because there was no other force in the universe. Perhaps the greatest example of this Hebrew belief was the attribution of the great flood to God. The thinking was simple. If something happened, God had to have done it. Thus the census, though viewed as evil by later religious teachers, was initially attributed to God.

Our final example involves as far-fetched a fable as anything found in Greek or Roman mythology. It is the story in

Genesis 6 of the "sons" of God (And you Christians thought there was only one!) coming down from heaven to take human wives. The result was a race of giants, descendants of which can still be seen, says the author. That's one way to explain the size of some of the guys in the NFL, but honestly, even the most ardent fundamentalist has a hard time explaining this one. The truth is that despite one's interest in preserving the integrity of the scriptures, this embarrassing mythological fragment slipped through the cracks. It never should have made it into the Hebrew canon.

If the Bible isn't inerrant or infallible, then what is it? Is it reliable? Authoritative?

As a religious—as opposed to mathematic or scientific—text, the bible most certainly is authoritative and is viewed as such by millions. Its great moral teachings, such as the Ten Commandments and the Golden Rule, have stood the test of time. Its teachings about God—that he demands justice yet offers forgiveness when we fail—squares with what our sagest scholars and saints have taught us for centuries. But it would be dishonest to tell you that every word of every chapter of the Bible is God's word for today. Few of us would defend those verses that admonish slaves to submit to their masters or the Psalmist's shocking praise for those who dash the babies of Israel's enemies against the rocks. Jesus taught us that God sends the rain on the just and the unjust alike and that all children are innocent and deserving of love.

Clergy respond to such glitches in the otherwise sterling revelation of God found in the Bible in a variety of ways. Most simply ignore them. Others invoke the doctrine of "progressive revelation"—the notion that God's revelation of himself has progressed over time in accordance with humans' progressive ability to understand. But, of course, this begs the question. It is, after all, only *humans'* understanding of God that has been recorded in the scriptures. The authors were men, not angels. If they understood God wrongly, most likely they recorded it wrongly.

The better approach would seem to be a frank acknowledgment that the biblical writers occasionally got it wrong. The Apostle Paul may be saying this very thing in the verse that is usually translated, "All scripture is inspired by God and is profitable for teaching, reproof, correction, and training in righteousness." The Greek text could just as easily be interpreted, "All scripture *that is inspired by God* is profitable for teaching..."

The purists among us are thrown into a tizzy by such an approach. Who can be trusted to determine which scripture is authoritative and which is not? On the surface, it appears that if any of the Bible is unreliable, it's all unreliable. *On the surface.*

The truth is that every weekend thousands of clergy stand in the pulpits of America and offer their version of what God's message is for today. Consciously or unconsciously, they steer clear of those passages they do not consider appropriate, helpful, or relevant. Face it—how long has it been since you heard a sermon advocating the death penalty for adulterers, Sabbath breakers (remember, the Sabbath is really Saturday!), or rebellious children? How many times have you seen women chased from God's house because they were menstruating or men excluded because of their physical handicaps? Yet all this and more is in the Bible.

The Bible is best understood as the effort of inspired writers to bear witness to God's acts in history as best they understood them at the time. The simple fact is that we may better understand God's will today than did the ancients before us. Is that surprising? We know more about science, medicine, and music. Why not more about God?

The notion that humankind's understanding of God has deepened or progressed shouldn't unsettle us. To the contrary, it should be cause for celebration. All religious teaching is a matter of faith, which by definition requires some degree of speculation. Who's to say that a thousand years from now some of our own interpretations about God and the Bible won't be revised or rejected? I would be surprised if they weren't. As one biblical writer put it, "Faith is the substance of things hoped for, the evidence of things un-seen." We shall always be groping as fallible humanity seeks to understand an infallible God.

If faith is what it takes to become a Christian, we shouldn't get rattled that it takes faith (and discernment) to interpret the Bible. For Christians, that means interpreting everything we read in light of the teachings of Jesus. Do that and your chances of misinterpreting the Bible are slim. Miss that and you might as well throw your Bible away.

After all, it's only a book.

✦ 4 ✦

Is There Really Such a Thing As a Miracle?

Miracle—just say the word, and our hearts quicken. We wonder. We hope. We yearn.

Living in the scientific age, we can't help but be skeptical. So when others tell us about some friend who has been healed, naturally we doubt. Yet when we're alone with our problems, who hasn't prayed for a miracle of her own?

If we're honest with ourselves, we'll admit there are things we simply don't understand. Ask any doctor with wrinkles, and he'll tell you a story or two that defies everything we know about medical science.

Take one of my old seminary professors. Maybe the brightest—and most skeptical—of the bunch. After being diagnosed with advanced prostate cancer and told that he had only six months to live, he decided to pray. Not for healing, mind you, but simply to thank God for seventy good years of life. "When I got up from my prayers," he recounted to me later, "I knew I had been healed." The next day he went back to see his doctor and insisted on paying for a second diagnostic test. Sure enough, the cancer was gone. You explain it.

Harvard's Stephen Jay Gould used to remind us that with a cranial capacity of only 1,500 cubic centimeters there were mysteries of the universe that were simply beyond a human's ability to understand. Modern man with all his hubris isn't used to thinking like that, but imagine, for example, trying to explain Euclidean geometry to your dog. You could talk until both of you start chasing your tails, but he'll never compute the area of a triangle.

Still, it's a cop-out for us not to try to understand the world around us. We may not be able to explain everything that passes under the label of miracle, but we certainly can draw *some* conclusions about miracles and their relationship to religious faith.

Before beginning, we need to take account of the wide variety of literary forms that are contained in the Bible. There are sagas, short stories, legends, myths, and poetry—many of which were never intended to be taken literally. A talking snake, for example, would surely qualify as a miracle until you realize that the writer of *Genesis* never intended that it be taken literally. It's a myth: a made-up story meant to make a point, namely, that God created a pristine world but evil found a way to intrude. Similarly, the prophet Elisha probably never made that axe head float on the water, but it's the sort of story people told to make the point that this man was different. George Washington probably didn't throw a dollar across the Potomac, either, but the legend underscored an important fact about our first president. He was strong. The point is that many of the "miraculous" details of our Bible stories, including the fish swallowing Jonah, weren't intended as historical accounts. Jonah is a parody on Jewish nationalism and exclusivism, not the anatomy of a whale.

Still, there are stories in the Bible that the writers no doubt intended be taken literally. The great miracles of the Exodus are prime examples. The crossing of the Red Sea, the provision of manna (meaning literally "What is it?") from heaven, and the fall of Jericho. The interesting thing, though, is that none of these so-called miracles may have violated the laws of nature. On the contrary, each may be explained in purely natural ways.

Take, for example, the crossing of the Red Sea. Legend has it that when Moses stretched out his rod, the seas parted and the Hebrew people walked across on dry land. When the Pharaoh's army tried to follow, the waters rushed back in, and they were drowned.

But the Bible never says that. It says the Hebrews crossed the "Sea of Reeds." The Sea of Reeds was a marshy area near the edge of the Mediterranean where dramatic shifts in tide were prone to occur. More than a few archaeologists have opined that after the Hebrews escaped, the pursuing Egyptian chariots became mired in the mud. An unusually high tide resulted in many of the trapped charioteers being drowned. The scriptural account may bear this out when it says that the water was driven back by a "strong east wind."

So did it happen as Charlton Heston portrayed it, or are the archaeologists closer to the truth? Good theology would suggest that it really doesn't matter. God may work in dramatic, supernatural ways as some believe, or he may work solely within the confines of the natural order he created. Either is miraculous in the eyes of the faithful.

Scholars make a similar point about the other miracles of the Exodus. Did God really send manna from heaven, or were the biblical writers referring to the honeydew-like secretions of two insects common in the region? The manna in the Bible is, after all, described as fine, sweet, and flaky—a perfect description of the secretions. And what about those walls of Jericho that the old spirituals say "came a-tumbling down"? Did God literally knock them down, or did the design of the walls (they were probably made of wood) simply give way when all those people ran to look over the edge at this ragtag army of nomads shouting and blowing their horns? Again, to the faithful it might not matter.

The point here is that what makes something a miracle is not a suspension of the laws of nature. What makes an event miraculous is the hand of God. A strong wind may or may not be a miracle. The same could be said for a much-needed rain. To many scientists, gene mutation and the emergence of a new species are miraculous. And who among us hasn't felt awed by the miracle of life as we stood outside a hospital nursery and stared at the newborn babies inside? Miracles are in the eye of the beholder. They can only be seen through the eyes of faith.

In the New Testament, miracle stories abound. Again, some may be intended as literal, historical accounts while others may not. Ancient religions brimmed with stories of virgin births, healings, and even bodily resurrections. Are Christian accounts materially different, or are they only intended to portray their founder as more than equal to Osiris, Adonis, or other ancient deities about whom similar stories were told?

Clearly, the writers of the Bible intended to portray Jesus as the Messiah, God's one-of-a-kind messenger sent to show us the way to salvation. Yet it's hard for any modern-day American to believe Jesus literally walked on water once we learn that similar stories were told about other great prophets and teachers of the ancient world.

My favorite analysis of a Christian miracle story came from my youngest daughter, who was five at the time. She was recounting what she had learned in Sunday School. "Jesus took all these people up on a mountain to teach them, *five thousand* of them," she said, "and they *got hungry*. So they looked around for some food, and all they could find was this little boy with five loaves and two fishes." She paused. "Dad, you're never going to believe this…Jesus tore that food into such little tiny pieces that everybody got a bite!"

See what I mean? Miracles are in the eyes of the beholder. What's more is you don't have to believe in the suspension of the laws of nature to be a person of faith. The greatest faith may well belong to the ones who cling to God when the miracles *don't* come. It's easy to believe in a miracle-working God.

The only prerequisite for entrance into the kingdom of God is not whether you believe in miracles. According to Jesus, it's whether you fed the hungry, clothed the naked, and attended to the needs of the "least of these."

Authentic religion is not a theology test. It's a love test.

· 5 ·

How Do I Please God?

He must have weighed three hundred pounds, even without his legs. Bearded and besotted, he was perched in that rank no-man's-land between the sidewalk and the pavement on America's most notorious street—Bourbon Street.

His arms were muscled from having to double as legs. Between the stumps where his legs should have been sat a can of beer. There were empties off to the side. Even the pickled brains of inebriated tourists sensed the danger. They gave him a wide berth.

That's the man, I said to myself. *That's the one God wants me to witness to.* I walked right up.

"Excuse me, sir," I said as I bent down and extended the gospel tract I was holding in my hand. "Could I talk with you? You know God loves you and has a wonderful plan for your life."

The man was on me like a snake. His meaty hand caught my shirt at the collar and pulled me down into the stench of his breath, down into the dank gutter. I watched in horror as the other hand reached in his pocket and pulled out a knife. He flicked it open and held it against my throat. Until then I had been squirming like a bug caught under a chicken's foot, but when I felt the steel on my exposed throat, I stopped moving.

"You damn Christians," he spat. "You come down here with your tickets to heaven telling drunks like me how much you love us and how much God loves us, but you don't really care. You're just a bunch of hypocrites. I'm an alcoholic. I'm homeless. And I need a place to sleep tonight. Which one of you preacher boys is going to take me home?"

Thus began the real theological education of Buzz Thomas. Not at the hands of a learned minister or rabbi, but at the hands of a bum. But as surely as God spoke through Balam's donkey more than two millennia ago, he was speaking to me that day. It would be years before I had the courage to take someone into my home, but my Bourbon Street buddy was right. Being religious isn't the same as being Christian, and satisfying the dictates of a religion may not satisfy God.

So what does it take to please God?

Different religions provide different answers. For Muslims, there are the Five Pillars of Islam. For Buddhists, the Seven Noble Truths. For Christians and Jews, their scriptures are a starting point, but interpretations of those scriptures vary widely depending upon the perspective of the particular religious teacher. Although portions of the Jewish and Christian scriptures overlap, the differences are profound. Simply put, being a good Christian and being a good Jew are similar in some ways and different in others. For that reason, we will confine our discussion to the tradition from which I, and presumably most of our readers, come—Christianity.

A measure of humility is in order here. This is *one* Christian view, not *the* Christian view. The pope's view on these matters, for example, is one that ought to be considered. So in my opinion is Billy Graham's. Beyond the fact that there are numerous Christian perspectives, there is at least the possibility that *we could all be wrong!* We don't think we are; otherwise, we wouldn't be Christians. But, when it comes to matters of the spirit, we're kidding ourselves if we fail to acknowledge that we are all speculating. Remember, dear pilgrims, these things can't be proved. That's why we call it *faith*. None of us should ever be so arrogant, for example, to pronounce that God doesn't hear the prayers of Muslims, Jews, or any other faith group. Our opinions notwithstanding, what God does and doesn't do is entirely up to God.

Although entry into the Christian life has been reduced by many to a simple formula for spiritual success, serious students of the New Testament are struck by the multitude of answers Jesus gave to those who came to him looking for salvation. To one person he said, "You know the commandments. Do these, and you shall live." To another, he offered the ethereal notion made famous by President Jimmy Carter, "You must be born again." To one of the thieves crucified alongside Jesus, a simple request to be remembered elicited these unforgettable words, "Today, you shall be with me in paradise." Jesus told a wealthy young official that he must sell everything he had and give it to the poor. At one point, Jesus even told a crowd, "No one can be my disciple who does not give up all of his possessions!" When was the last time you heard that preached from the pulpit?

The inescapable conclusion is that there is no single answer to religion's most vexing question. The road to salvation depends upon who's standing in the road. And, just as important, what's standing between that person and God. If it's riches, surely they must go, but the same could be said of pride, excessive devotion to work, or a smug self-righteousness—a common malady among the religious in Jesus' day as well as in our own. What stands between an individual and God depends upon the individual. Jesus does seem to be saying as a threshold matter, however, that obedience to the will of God should be every person's top priority.

But now we're back to where we started. What does it mean to be obedient to the will of God?

To answer that question, let's start with the New Testament's most prolific writer—the Apostle Paul. Nearly half the New Testament was written by Paul, and without him it's likely that Christianity never would have penetrated the Greco-Roman world.

To put Paul's teachings in context, consider that before becoming a Christian missionary, he was a devout Jew. A "Pharisee of the Pharisees," as he put it, Paul was devout in every way. So zealous was he that as a young man Paul held the coats of those who stoned the first Christian martyr, Saint Stephen. Paul spent most of his life trying desperately to please God. He meticulously attended to every detail of the Jewish law and tried his best to attain a state of personal righteousness. Paul reminds us of the great reformer Martin Luther, who in his quest for spiritual purity finally resorted to beating himself!

Then Paul was converted. While traveling on the road to Damascus, he was struck blind by an unexplained light. Paul claimed it was the risen Christ. Although he regained his sight, Paul was never the same. Time-honored rituals such as circumcision and Sabbath observance were discarded. "Circumcise your hearts," said the former Pharisee. "That's all God cares about." Paul now dismissed the Jewish law that had consumed his early adulthood as little more than a temporary tutor to help one along the path to God.

In one of Paul's most memorable statements, he explained to the church at Ephesus the key to salvation: "By grace are you saved through faith. It is not a result of your own good works. It is the gift of God. Lest any person should boast" (Ephesians 2:8–9). Grace. The unconditional, unmerited favor of the deity.

How does one access this "amazing" grace? By honestly and sincerely asking for it. That's it, that's what faith is. As a preacher friend once said, "We're all bastards, but God loves us anyway."

What a revolutionary idea! Our failure to achieve moral perfection is not counted against us. All we must do is humbly acknowledge our shortcomings and receive the grace that is available to us all.

To some this sounds like an invitation to sin. If it all boils down to grace, why bother with being good? Just have faith and do as you please, right?

James, the brother of Jesus, responds to this dilemma in the New Testament book that bears his name. "Faith without works is dead," says James. In other words, any person who says he has faith but has no good works to show for it is a liar.

For those who sense a contradiction between the teachings of James and Paul, consider this. For Paul, good works are assumed. They aren't what saves us, but they are performed out of gratitude and obedience to the God who loves us. Most likely, Paul would have put it something like this: "Faith without works isn't really faith."

According to the Apostle Paul, faith is more than mere belief. It's not enough to believe that God through Christ has offered forgiveness to the world. True faith requires that we act upon that belief. Asking for forgiveness implies a willingness to turn from our past error and to begin walking in the other direction. That's what the word *repent* means—to turn around. Biblical faith is like an airplane. You may believe that the plane can take you to Hawaii, and you may sincerely want to go; but until you actually get on the plane, you won't be going.

Faith is saying to God, "I believe you care about me. I believe you want to forgive me and free me from the guilt, fear, and uncertainty that have plagued me. Here is my life. Take it, and help me to live it in a way that is pleasing to you."

That's it. That's all it takes to begin the journey of faith. The journey itself, of course, is more complicated. Volumes have been written on how to live as a faithful Christian. Certainly, Christians ought to pray, worship, read their Bibles, and join a church. A healthy church will supply members with at least two critical needs: community and an opportunity to serve. Humans are social creatures. Without the benefit of a support group, even the strongest among us lose heart. The same is true for service. Our wisest sages speak of the unparalleled satisfaction that comes from helping others. Anyone who has ever raised a child, taught someone to read, or comforted a grieving friend knows it is true. Healthy churches provide their members with opportunities to serve. Shelters, soup kitchens, thrift stores, day care centers, after-school programs, and medical clinics are just a few examples. But, there's more to the Christian life even than serving. There is, after all, living to be done. So what about the business of living?

Living a life pleasing to God is really more simple than it looks. To be perfectly honest, knowing what to do isn't so hard. Actually doing it, on the other hand, can be excruciating. As Mark Twain once put it, "It isn't the parts of the Bible I don't understand that trouble me. It's the parts that I do!"

Let's start with the basics. First, the Ten Commandments. Although Christians have been freed from the yoke of legalism, the Ten Commandments are a good barometer of whether our new life of grace is really working or has become more or less a license to sin.

Are there any false gods in our life? Money, status, fame, youth? Are we honest in our dealings with others? Do we cheat on our spouses, our business partners, or the IRS? Do we treat our parents with respect? You get the point. The

Ten Commandments are a good indicator of how we're doing in our effort to live lives pleasing to God.

But don't be fooled into the most pernicious sin of all—self-righteousness. None of us really keeps the commandments. Is there anyone of us who hasn't put something ahead of God? Very few Americans tithe (give 10 percent of their money to charity or the church), for example, and the Bible says that nontithers are "robbing" God. No kidding. But, here's the worst part. Jesus said that tithing isn't nearly enough. In the famous story of the widow's mite (i.e., penny), Jesus explained that the true test of our faith is not how much we give but how much we keep. Only the widow *who literally gave all that she had* is held up as a model of Christian stewardship.

Jesus went on to explain how other commandments are violated. You may not have committed adultery, he said, but if you have lusted after another person, you have committed adultery in your heart. Who hasn't done that? The same is true for the commandment against murder when we harbor grudges or wish ill on another person. The bottom line is simple. No one keeps all the commandments all the time. Not really. But the Ten Commandments do serve as a helpful guide for determining whether we are living lives pleasing to God.

Then there's the critical question of how we treat others—especially those less fortunate than ourselves. If the writers of the Bible have any credibility at all about the nature of God, we can be sure he has a special concern for the most vulnerable members of society. There are more verses about helping the poor, the elderly, widows, and orphans than there are about prayer, heaven, or the end of time.

Of course, the most vulnerable members of any society are its children, and the Bible is filled with verses about their welfare. Who can forget Jesus' rebuke to his disciples over their dismissive attitude toward a group of children who were clamoring for his attention? "Suffer the little children to come unto me for such is the kingdom of God!" said Jesus. It's a bad reflection on American Christianity that nearly a fourth of the nation's children live in poverty while two-thirds of its citizens claim membership in a church! And what of the fact that some ten million children subsist without health insurance? Many of these never see a doctor or dentist until their problems become serious enough to land them in the emergency room. So much for America's claimed identity as a "Christian" nation.

God's great acts in history are also an indication of his preference for the underdog. The climactic event of the Old Testament is God's intervention in human affairs through the person of Moses to deliver the children of Israel from slavery.

These "chosen" people were not a superpower of the ancient world, like the Greeks, Romans, or Egyptians. They were the nobodies, the never-had-beens. Ancient Israel was little more than a political football kicked around by the Assyrians, Babylonians, and Persians for centuries. Yet God chose this humble nation to become the bearer of his revelation to the world.

Similarly, God's great act in the New Testament—his intervention in history through the person of Jesus—was not what we would have predicted. If the God of the universe chose to reveal himself in human form, would he not choose someone rich and powerful? A king or emperor, perhaps? Instead, he chose an itinerant carpenter-turned-rabbi whose peasant mother was so poor she couldn't even afford the lamb for her purification ceremony! She bought two pigeons instead. And on one occasion, when her son offered his followers a glimpse at what the final judgment would be like, he said the proof of our faith would be whether we had fed the hungry, clothed the naked, visited prisoners, and welcomed strangers. If we are not doing those things, Jesus said, we have drifted from authentic faith to a superficial religiosity that cannot save.

These ideas weren't new, of course. Jesus got them from his Jewish upbringing. The Hebrew prophets had railed against the indifference of the wealthy to the plight of the poor. In one of his most memorable sermons, the Prophet

Isaiah insisted that instead of praying and fasting, the Hebrews should share their bread and take the homeless poor into their houses. Sound familiar?

Of course, there is more to the life of faith than caring for the poor. The Sermon on the Mount—considered by many to be the pinnacle of Jesus' ethical teachings—instructs us to love our enemies, repay evil with good, refrain from judging others, shun evil thoughts, and never make a show of our religion. That should keep us busy for a while.

If this is beginning to sound complicated, relax. Jesus once provided a summary of all religious teachings in two pithy commandments: Love God and love your neighbor. When a clever lawyer asked him who was our neighbor, Jesus answered with the timeless parable of the good Samaritan. Who is your neighbor? Anyone in need.

Near the end of his life, Jesus raised the bar one last time. He instructed his followers to love one another "as I have loved you." The implication is startling, really, but it cannot be avoided if we are to remain true to the teachings of our founder and the one by whose name we are called. As the great Lutheran theologian Deitrich Bonhoeffer put it, Christians are called to come and die: to give our lives away in service to others.

If this all sounds daunting, it is. Few of us will ever attain the level of obedience to the will of God that was revealed in Christ. But we needn't despair. When we fail to measure up, the promise of grace remains.

Martin Luther said it best: Make peace with God and sin on bravely.

· 6 ·

What About Women?

◆

Nothing roots out male chauvinism like the birth of a daughter. By the time a little boy in my daughter's preschool told her she couldn't play with the toy trucks because "they weren't for girls," I was a raging feminist. Later when a Sunday school teacher told her she couldn't be a minister "even if God calls you," I thought I was going to have a stroke. Even today, I'm surprised all over again when I consider that despite constituting more than half the members of the church (Not to mention doing 90 percent of the work!), women continue to take a backseat to their male counterparts. After two thousand years, it is still true that the world's largest Christian organization has not ordained a single woman into the priesthood.

Why? And, more important, does the Bible justify the church's shabby treatment of women?

For answers, let's start with the New Testament's two most familiar passages on the role of women. Both were written by Saint Paul, and both have served to justify what any modern-day court would consider illegal sex discrimination. What makes it permissible for religious organizations is the First Amendment. The separation of church and state shields religious organizations from intrusive government regulation, including regulation of their hiring practices. If Americans wish to associate themselves with religious organizations that practice sex discrimination, so be it: the U.S. Constitution won't stand in the way. On balance, that's a good thing. Religious freedom is, after all, a fundamental part of the American arrangement. But allowing it and liking it are two different things. I hope there's something inside every American that is offended anytime discrimination takes place. Especially in the name of religion.

Now for those verses.

"Be subject to one another out of reverence for Christ. Wives, be subject to your husbands as to the Lord. For the husband is the head of the wife as Christ is the head of the church." (Ephesians 5:21–23)

"Let a woman learn in silence with all submissiveness. I permit no woman to teach or to have authority over men; she is to keep silent." (I Timothy 2:11–12)

On the surface, these verses seem to give a clear explanation of the role of women in both the home and in the church. Wives are to submit to their husbands, and no woman is to exercise authority over a man.

Simple, right?

Wrong. Remember that things aren't always what they seem when it comes to interpreting the Bible. The first rule of good biblical interpretation is always to examine the *historical context* in which a particular passage was written. If we don't know why the verse was written back then, we stand little chance of understanding what it means today.

The passages we just read were written in the first century to an audience of Jews, Romans, and Greeks. This was not the twenty-first century. It was the first.

First-century life was much like it had been for the previous millennium. That is to say, in most every ancient civilization, women had no rights. Under Hebrew law, a woman was a thing to be bought, sold, or coveted like a piece of property, almost like a goat. Old Testament laws against rape and adultery gave no recourse to the woman who was violated. Any fines that were levied against the perpetrator were paid to the woman's father, for he *owned* his daughter.

Marriages were business transactions, with a young woman being the commodity for which men bargained. Whether she brought fifty cattle or a thousand to the marriage, all women were treated as chattel. The only thing folks haggled about was the price.

Things were little better in Greece and Rome. Under Roman law, a woman had no rights. As a child, she belonged to her father; as an adult, to her husband. Both had the power of life and death over her. A wife was subject entirely to the whims of her husband. She could not so much as speak to a man without his permission. She was not allowed to drink wine. (Everybody knows what happens to a woman when she drinks wine, right?) According to the Roman statesman and general Cato, "If a husband catches his wife in an act of infidelity, he can kill her with impunity and without trial, but if a wife catches her husband, she cannot so much as lay a finger on him!"

Little wonder the Apostle Paul instructed women as he did, for no self-respecting Jew or Roman of the first century would allow a woman to teach him anything. A woman would have enjoyed the same reception as a slave or a child. Had a woman done other than submit to her husband, she could have been killed. In fact, it is remarkable that Paul gave women the recognition that he did. By first-century standards, he was a liberal. (Sorry, Ann Coulter, but not all liberals are "godless.")

In his letter to the Corinthians, Paul makes provision for women to prophesy (i.e., preach) in the church. In Romans, he sends greetings to his friend Phoebe, a deacon. And throughout his missionary journeys, he worked collegially with numerous women, some of whom the New Testament mentions by name (e.g., Euodia and Priscilla).

This unusual level of respect within the church for women didn't originate with Paul. Jesus had publicly associated with women—even outcast women such as prostitutes and Samaritans—at a time when no self-respecting rabbi would be caught dead conversing with a woman in public. The rabbis and priests barred women from the inner courts of the temple and prayed daily, "I thank thee, O Lord, that thou hast not made me a Gentile or a woman." Yet the New Testament records that when Jesus rose from the dead, the first person to whom he appeared was a woman.

No, the Apostle Paul was not giving the church license to dominate women. Nor was he telling women of the twenty-first century that they are second-class citizens who must bow and scrape to the whims of their husbands. Paul's ultimate hope for men and women was that there would be no distinctions. As he put it in his letter to the Galatians, "There is neither Jew nor Greek, slave nor free, male nor female, for you are all one in Christ Jesus." Now that's radical stuff.

The fact is that the church was once years ahead of its time in its treatment of women. While society was keeping women enslaved, the church was appointing them to positions of responsibility and leadership. Female deacons were prominent in the early church, their qualifications for office being set down in 1 Timothy 3:11. (Note: the Greek word often translated as "wives" is better translated as "women.") Female preachers were also commonplace. In the Acts of the Apostles, Luke speaks of Phillip's four daughters, all of whom were preachers. At the Council of Chalcedon in the fifth century, specific rules were laid down for the ordination of women, but soon after, male chauvinism reared its ugly head. Female deacons and preachers disappeared, and they would not return until the nineteenth century. Most have not returned even today.

Despite the overwhelming evidence to the contrary, some Christians still maintain that women cannot adequately serve as ministers. "The Bible says it, I believe it, and that settles it," goes their mantra.

The problem, of course, is that God will not be locked into the culture of the first century, whether we like it or not. If God exists, then, he is alive *today* and is continuing to reveal himself.

Nowhere is this better illustrated than with the subject of slavery. Slavery is assumed throughout the Bible. Not only is it assumed, it is actively encouraged! For example, Peter and Paul actually tell slaves to submit to their masters as to the Lord.

How can this be? Why would God's representatives promote an institution as heinous and hell-conceived as we now know slavery to be?

Two reasons. First, the apostles knew they weren't going to change the world overnight. Had they encouraged slaves to overthrow their masters, there would have been blood in the streets. Slave blood. Second, the apostles lived in a different place and time. It's madness to expect them to be anything other than the first-century people they were. In a word, they were *victims* of their culture, much as we are victims of our own. By definition, we cannot see our own blind spots, but we can see theirs.

Does the fact that Peter and Paul condoned slavery mean that slavery is all right today?

God forbid! Even the most literalistic interpreters of scripture concede that for one person to enslave another is sin. If God abhors anything, he abhors that. Yet during the nineteenth century, southerners like myself used the "word of God," as they liked to call the Bible, to justify their sin.

So, I ask the male leaders of our religious institutions today, will we do the same? The secular world is ready to give women equal rights. Will God's own people prevent it? As we quote proof texts written in the first century to people living in the twenty-first century, do we not sound like our southern forebears who tried to stop the abolitionist movement (and later the civil rights movement) by quoting the Bible?

Times change, and God's people must be prepared to change with those times. The time for men to lord authority over women is over, whether inside or outside the church. Instead, we should be working together as equals, for equals we surely are.

In light of my earlier observation—namely, that women do 90 percent of the work in most churches—I have a question. Ladies, have you considered a strike?

· 7 ·

What About Homosexuality?

I could overhear my daughter talking on the phone with her friend. The voices were hushed, but the sound of fear is unmistakable at any decibel level. I tuned in.

The boy's father, a respected businessman and Baptist deacon, had just learned that his son was gay. Years earlier, the mother had sensed her son's sexual orientation and offered support, but she was now dead. Outraged and alone, the father fell back on his fundamentalist Christian beliefs. *Homosexuality is an abomination...* He gave the boy an hour to pack his bags and leave.

Thus began my life as the temporary surrogate parent of a gay child. Though he only stayed with us for a few months (the boy and his father were later reconciled), I would be forever changed and so would my family. Gay rights was no longer just another worthwhile cause for us. It was personal.

So what would make a father reject his only son?

Religion. Pure and simple. Remember, it's one of the few things people will actually kill one another over. Indeed, a majority of the bloodiest conflicts in the world, including Al Qaida's war against the United States, has something to do with religion.

Many pastors have convinced their congregants that the Bible is unequivocal about homosexuality. Homosexuality, they say, is a sin, and anyone who so much as tolerates it is an aider and abettor. The nation's largest Protestant denomination took this so far as to *boycott Disneyworld* for providing health benefits to gay and lesbian employees. (We can only hope they're loving their *straight* neighbors as themselves!)

So, is homosexuality a sin? Is that what the Bible really says?

Certainly the writer of Leviticus thought so. As he put it, "You shall not lie with a man as with a woman. It is an abomination" (Leviticus 18:22). Simple? Sure, but remember what Einstein said. There is a simple answer for everything, and it's usually wrong.

The book of Leviticus is filled with laws imposing the death penalty on everything from eating catfish to sassing your parents. If you're going to accept one as the absolute, unequivocal word of God, you'd better be prepared to accept them all. As you may be starting to imagine, the results would be unthinkable. To make the point, I'll turn to an unattributed open letter that was sent to conservative radio talk show host Dr. Laura Schlessinger, and posted on the Internet. The listener asked Dr. Laura:

1. When I burn a bull on the altar as a sacrifice (remember, sacrifices are mandatory), I know it creates a pleasing odor for the Lord. (Leviticus 1:9) The problem is my neighbors. They claim the odor is not pleasing to them. Should I smite them?

2. I would like to sell my daughter into slavery as sanctioned in Exodus 21:7. In this day and age, what do you think would be a fair price for her?

3. I know that I am allowed no contact with a woman during her period of menstrual uncleanliness. (Leviticus 15:19–24) The problem is, how do I tell? I've tried asking, but most women take offense.

4. Leviticus 25:44 states that I may indeed possess slaves, both male and female, provided they are purchased from neighboring nations. A friend of mine claims this applies to Mexicans but not Canadians? Can you clarify? Why can't I own Canadians?

5. I have a neighbor who insists on working on the Sabbath (literally Saturday). Exodus 35:2 clearly states that

he should be put to death. Am I morally obligated to kill him myself? Must I also kill his offspring?

6. Eating shellfish is an abomination. Leviticus 11:10. Is it a lesser abomination than homosexuality? Can you settle this?

7. Leviticus 21:20 states that I may not approach the altar of God if I have a defect in my sight. I have to admit that I wear reading glasses. Does my vision have to be 20/20, or is there some wiggle room here?

8. Most of my male friends get their hair trimmed, including the hair around the temples, even though this is expressly forbidden by Leviticus 19:27. How should they die?

9. I know from Leviticus 11:6–8 that touching the skin of a dead pig makes me unclean, but may I still play football if I wear gloves?

10. My uncle has a farm. He violates Leviticus 19:19 by planting two different crops in the same field, as does his wife by wearing garments made of two different kinds of thread (cotton/polyester blend). He also tends to curse and blaspheme a lot. Is it really necessary that we go to all the trouble of getting the whole town together to stone them? Leviticus 24:10–16. Couldn't we just burn them to death at a private family affair like we do with people who sleep with their in-laws? Leviticus 20:14.

The truth is that mainstream religion moved beyond animal sacrifice, slavery, and the host of primitive rituals described in Leviticus centuries ago. Selectively hanging onto these ancient proscriptions for gays and lesbians exclusively is unfair according to anybody's standard of ethics. Lawyers call it "selective enforcement," and in civil affairs it's illegal.

A better reading of Hebrew scripture starts with the book of Genesis and the grand pronouncement about the world God created and all those who dwelled in it: "And, the Lord saw that it was good" (Genesis 1:31). That's especially important given what we now know about a person's sexual orientation and how it comes to be. The best science and countless testimonials from homosexuals themselves suggest that sexual orientation is *not* a matter of choice. It's a matter of genetics, brain structure, or the mother's hormones. Simply put, people are born gay and lesbian. As more than one gay person has told me, "Who in their right mind would choose this?!" For many, it is a life in the shadows, if not one of outright ostracism and pain. For others, it is a life of constant medication and endless trips to the doctor. For all gay people, it is a struggle swimming against the inexorable tide of what society considers "normal."

But if God created us and if everything he created is good, how can a gay person be guilty of being anything more than what God created him to be? Viewed in this light, society's current intolerance toward homosexuals starts to look more like the racism of the Ku Klux Klan or the anti-Semitism of Nazi Germany rather than authentic biblical faith. We'd do well to remember that both the Klan and the Nazis used proof texts from the Bible to support their prejudices.

In the New Testament, the writings of the Apostle Paul at first seem to give credence to the ancient Levitical notion that homosexuality is indeed an abomination to God. In his letter to the Romans, Paul speaks of men exchanging their natural passions for those that are unnatural and committing "shameless acts" with other men. "God has given them up," Paul continues, "to a base mind and to improper conduct" (Rom. 1:26).

Again, it all sounds clear until you consider that Paul is probably speaking here about the Roman practice of *pederasty*, a form of pedophilia that was common in the ancient world. Successful older men often took young boys into their homes as concubines, lovers, or sexual slaves. In today's world, such sexual exploitation of minors is no longer tolerated. Instead, we send the perpetrators of such crimes to prison for lengthy sentences. The point is that the sort of long-term, committed same-sex relationships that are being debated today were unheard of in the New Testament. It distorts the biblical witness to apply verses written in one historical context (i.e., the sexual exploitation of children) to contemporary situations between two monogamous partners of the same sex. Sexual promiscuity is condemned by the Bible whether it be among gays or straights. Sexual fidelity is not.

Which brings us to the question of marriage. If the Bible doesn't condemn monogamous homosexual relations, why don't we allow gays to marry?

The reasons most often cited are procreation and social stability. Only heterosexuals can procreate, goes the first argument, so biology itself stands against gay marriage. Interesting, but if procreation were our sole concern, we wouldn't allow the elderly to marry or, for that matter, the infertile. But we do, of course, because marriage is about much more than procreation. Partnership, not procreation, is the primary feature of marriage.

The social stability argument also starts to fall apart when you examine it closely—embarrassingly so, in fact. The argument goes something like this. The traditional heterosexual family is the basic building block of society. Undermine that and you undermine everything.

In reality, the people undermining the family aren't the relative handful of gay couples lining up to marry; it's the multitude of heterosexual couples lining up to divorce! Fifty percent of heterosexual marriages now end in divorce, and a large percentage of those remaining are wracked by infidelity. Some of our most celebrated citizens have been married as many as eight times, and thousands of ordinary Americans still practice plural marriage. I'm not talking about the wife swappers—just those with multiple husbands or wives.

I hope you're starting to sense the irony here. Would we rather encourage committed, monogamous relationships that are stable or the unstable, promiscuous relationships so common in the gay community? It should be a no-brainer for a family-oriented society such as our own. Remember, gay marriage doesn't create more gay people—just more stable gay relationships. That's the real social stability argument.

The only thing left remaining is the problem of language. Marriage is defined as the union of a man and a woman in the bonds of matrimony. Change that definition, and it becomes something other than marriage.

Fine. What we're really talking about here is not semantics. It's the bundle of rights and responsibilities that attach to the traditional marriage covenant. (One writer has identified more than a thousand!) The point is that no citizen should be denied access to those benefits. Whether we call these relationships civil unions or domestic partnerships is beside the point. The important thing is that citizens be allowed to covenant together in stable, long-term relationships. (Given that marriage relationships were conceived and instituted by religious communities and that the First Amendment separates church and state, the state probably should treat all such covenants as civil unions, be they homosexual or heterosexual, and leave the determination of whether such a relationship qualifies as a "marriage" to the religious institutions themselves.)

For those who have lingering doubts, I suggest you dust off your Bible and reacquaint yourself with the teachings of Jesus. Try as you may, you won't find a single reference to homosexuality. There are teachings on money, lust, revenge, divorce, prayer, fasting, and a thousand other subjects (with an especially large number on self-righteousness), but there is nothing on homosexuality. Strange, don't you think, if it were such a threat to the moral order?

On the other hand, Jesus did spend a lot of time talking about how we should treat others. First, he made clear it is not our role to judge. It is God's. ("Judge not lest you be judged," [Matthew 7.1].) Second, he commanded us to love other people *as we love ourselves.*

So, I ask you: Would you want to be discriminated against? Would you want to lose your job, housing, or insurance benefits because of something over which you had no control? Better yet, would you like it if society told you that you couldn't visit your lifelong partner in the hospital or file a claim on his behalf if he were murdered?

Sometimes theology can get complicated and the answers hard to come by.

Not this time.

· 8 ·

What About Other Faiths?

Carl Sandburg was once asked what was the dirtiest word in the English language. His answer still turns heads. "Exclusive," said America's most popular poet of the twentieth century. That's the dirtiest word of all.

Humans are innately social animals. The upside of this is we are adept at forming associations; the downside is we are adept at forming associations. We like to exclude.

We do it variously. From the WHITES ONLY signs of yesteryear to today's country clubs and gated communities, from groups like the Crips and Bloods to Sigma Chi and Chi Omega. Humans have an insatiable desire to label, categorize, pigeonhole and, ultimately, exclude. Us versus them.

Religions, unfortunately, are among the worst offenders. What's more, religious claims aren't easily challenged on the basis of logic or rational thought. Religion, after all, is a matter of revelation. If God said it, there's not much room for debate.

The exclusive claims of religion, though reassuring to some, raise unsettling questions for others. Who among us hasn't wondered what happens to those who don't share our religious beliefs? Even more troubling, what about those whose beliefs are different yet who manage to live exemplary, or even inspiring, moral lives? Finally, what of those who have never even heard of our particular religion and, therefore, lack the opportunity to respond? Does God cut them any slack, or are they headed down the tubes with the rest of the unbelievers? Even worse, what if *they* are right, and *we* are wrong? Ever consider that possibility? Fortunately, the Bible offers some insight.

At the outset, we probably ought to address the question of whether Judaism's and Christianity's claims are as exclusive as some might have thought. For the reader of the Hebrew scriptures, certainly there is the claim that the God of Abraham, Issac, and Jacob is the only true God. But having said that, we must remind ourselves that in addition to Judaism at least two other world religions—Christianity and Islam—share this belief. The two also consider themselves children of Abraham, and as such they worship Abraham's God. They also pray, fast, give alms, seek justice, and practice charity much the same as most observant Jews do. It's worth noting that modern Judaism, at least as it is practiced in the United States, does not seek to convert Christians and Muslims. Judaism is one of those religions that is open for business but not out soliciting.

Contrast that with Christianity, which is one of the world's most aggressive faiths. The book of Matthew ends with Jesus instructing his followers to "make disciples of all nations." Certainly, Christians have taken this so-called great commission seriously, given that we employ thousands of missionaries at home and abroad for the sole purpose of winning converts.

It is not at all clear, however, that Jesus considered all non-Christians to be in need of conversion. Consider his numerous admonitions to inquiring Jews, as recorded in the New Testament. To some he said simply, "You know the commandments. Do these and you shall live." To others, he suggested more would be required, such as shedding their material possessions or leaving family and friends. To one who came asking, "Good teacher, what must I do to inherit eternal life," he gave this memorable response: "Good? You call me good? There is none good but God!" When one of Jesus' disciples sought to identify him as the long-awaited messiah, Mark's gospel records that Jesus rebuked him and instructed him to tell no one. Rarely, if ever, did Jesus tell audiences that in order to please God they had to "accept him as their personal lord and savior," which is evangelical Christianity's standard line.

Jesus seemed to have an uncanny sense of knowing who needed converting and who did not. To those overly zealous Jews who traveled widely in their efforts to win converts—in a manner somewhat reminiscent of today's Christian missionaries—Jesus had a particularly harsh retort: "You cross land and sea to make one convert in order to make him twice the son of hell that you are!" (Matthew 23:15). Jesus was much more interested, it seems, in simplifying religion's demands to two simple commandments: Love God, and love your neighbor (something many missionaries have given their lives to). One needn't be a Christian to do that.

There's more to it, of course. Shortly after Jesus' death, Christians elevated the Christian message to a more exclusive one. The preaching of the apostles began to suggest there was no other path to God except through Christ. The Gospel according to John, recorded nearly two generations after Jesus' death, goes so far as to attribute such a claim to Jesus himself: "I am the way, the truth and the life. No man comes to the Father except through me" (John 14:6). Though it sounds familiar to Christian ears, the statement is so uncharacteristic of Jesus' own preaching that it is found in none of the earlier gospels, leaving the reader to speculate, along with a host of biblical scholars, whether it was a later addition. We have already seen that the writer of John's gospel took liberties with other details of the gospel story, including the date of Jesus' crucifixion and the events surrounding his resurrection.

Even the Apostle Paul is not entirely clear that all non-Christians were in need of conversion. Certainly, he railed against the legalisms of first-century Judaism, including any false notion that personal righteousness could be obtained through obedience to the law. But at the same time, he cited Jews such as Abraham and Elijah (who had never even heard of Jesus, much less professed faith in him) as heroes of God. Paul's primary argument is that salvation comes by the grace of God through faith. Because Jesus was the best first-century vehicle for conveying that message, Paul preached Jesus.

Suppose I'm wrong and that both Jesus and Paul intended the Christian message to be exclusive. In other words, no Jesus, no salvation. Where does that leave us? Certainly, it motivates the church to engage in missions and evangelism. But with that motivation must come a deep respect for the right of others to say no. Not because it's politically correct, but because God requires it. Being made "in the image of God," as the Hebrew scriptures describe it, means that humans are free—free to choose for or against God. And, being free means that we are "response-able," as Wake Forest Divinity School professor James Dunn likes to put it. In other words, we come to God voluntarily or not really. Coerced religion is an oxymoron, kind of like jumbo shrimp. If the church is to bear witness to an *exclusive* claim, it must do so with an attitude of tolerance for those who decline the invitation.

But what about Jesus' statement in Matthew 10:34 that he came "not to bring peace but a sword"?

The point is that Jesus' message requires a choice. And given the radical nature of that choice (i.e., "No person can be my disciple who does not give up all his possessions.... No person can be my disciple who does not deny himself daily, take up his cross and follow me!" [Luke 14:26–33].), it is no surprise that Jesus would warn of the inevitable conflict with colleagues, family members, and society itself.

The fact that the decision to follow Jesus was intended to be a radical one with life-altering consequences did not lead Jesus to manipulate or coerce. To the contrary, Jesus seemed to actively discourage mass conversions. He warned audiences to count the cost of discipleship and rebuked those who publicly sought to proclaim him messiah. At no point did Jesus pressure his audiences, and he never once solicited financial support—proof positive that Jesus would have failed miserably as a modern televangelist!

In short, the Christian gospel, although radical, was not militant. Christians existed peacefully alongside Jews, Stoics, Epicureans, pagans, and other religious groups for centuries. Only after Emperor Constantine's conversion in the fourth century did Christianity become coercive. This unholy union of church and state spawned years of blood-shed, culminating in the crusades and inquisitions of the Middle Ages. Militant Islam responded in kind, and the groundwork was laid for the conflict between East and West that persists until this day.

If humans are to live together with their deepest differences, tolerance will not be optional; it will be required. Just look around the world today, and you can't help but note that most of our bloodiest conflicts have something to do with religion. Think of Northern Ireland, Eastern Europe, the Sudan, and the Middle East. While we shouldn't necessarily expect people to respect beliefs or practices with which they disagree (I don't respect, for example, the belief that women are somehow religiously inferior to men), we must respect the *right* of people to choose those beliefs. Tolerance is the ticket—the only ticket, if we're to survive as a species.

Think of it this way: Failure to protect anyone's right to religious freedom diminishes everyone's religious freedom.

Have I mentioned that I'm a fan of Carl Sandburg?

+ 9 +

What Happens After We Die?

*If you who are evil know how to give good things to
your children, how much more will your Father who is
in heaven give good things to those who ask him.*

—*MATTHEW 7:11*

＋

Imagine a judge who sentenced a jaywalker to life in prison. Better yet, imagine one who imposed the death penalty on a troubled kid who had a habit of skipping school. Such a judge would be reversed by every appellate court in the land and run out of office at the next election—that is, if the legislature didn't impeach him first. Yet these judges would be lenient compared to the one who would impose an eternity of horrific suffering on hapless souls who fail to adopt a particular set of religious beliefs.

Each Sunday, millions of Christians are taught that (1) God is love, and (2) failure to obey God will land you in a place of everlasting torment.

Having trouble putting the two things together?

The truth is that neither Jesus nor the Hebrew prophets

preached a literal burning hell of the sort imagined by me-dieval Catholic theologians or taught in thousands of evan-gelical churches today.

For the Jewish people, notions of everlasting punish-ment never took hold. True, an eye-for-an-eye justice could be harsh, but for the ancient Hebrews once you were dead, you were dead.

The Hebrew scriptures speak of a place called Sheol where all persons—good and evil—went when they died. Sheol was thought to be a kind of drab, uneventful, dream-like place, not too different from sleep. As the writer of Proverbs put it, "Whatever your hand finds to do, do it with your might for there is no activity in Sheol where you are ultimately going!" Admittedly, it's not the most pleasant-sounding existence, but compared to everlasting torment you can see its appeal. In all seriousness, the Hebrew people should be commended for developing a religion that is life affirming rather than life denying. In short, Judaism is about the here and now. Little thought or anxiety is given to what happens after we die. Just do what you're supposed to be doing while you're here on earth, and trust God to handle the rest. I like that.

The Christian scriptures take a different slant. They em-body a dualistic approach originating with the ancient Persians—one of rewards for the good guys and punish-ment for the bad.

For the followers of Christ, there is heaven. It is variously described as a place of eternal happiness, unmatched beauty, and supreme contentment. It is to be so glorious, in fact, that the biblical writers strain to describe it. Streets of gold, gates of pearl, a crystal sea…in heaven, there is to be no pain, no tears, and no unhappiness. Most important, it's where God is.

In Jesus' most famous teaching on the afterlife, he reinforced this notion of being present with God. "In my Father's house are many dwelling places," he said in John's gospel. That's winning the big quinella, isn't it—being present with a loving God for eternity? And then there's the ineffable satisfaction that comes from a life well lived. In one of Jesus' more famous parables, he identified the words that all humans long to hear when they finish their earthly stay: "Well done, thou good and faithful servant. Enter the rest that has been prepared for you."

There's your heaven. God's validation that our lives have had purpose and meaning. Imagine the peace that comes with that. I'll take that over pearly gates and streets of gold any day.

Interestingly, Jesus didn't talk much about heaven. More often he spoke within his Jewish tradition of the joyful life that is available *now* to those who follow his teachings. The word used to describe this kind of life, though commonly translated "eternal," is better understood as a measure of quality, not quantity. One saying attributed to Jesus captures it best: "I came that you might have life and have it more abundantly!"

So we know what happens to the good guys. They're supposed to have abundant life now and perhaps forever. What happens to the bad guys is a little less clear. Virtually every reference to hell that comes from the lips of Jesus is a mistranslation. The word translated as *hell* by the King James Bible is the Greek word *Gehenna*, literally "the valley of the sons of Hinnom." This notorious valley to the south of Jerusalem had been the site of pagan sacrifices, including child sacrifice, in ancient times and had long been cursed by the prophets of Israel. By Jesus' day, it served as the garbage dump for the city. It was a foul, noxious place where dogs roamed and fires burned continually as the city struggled to eliminate its trash before the days of compressors and hydraulic shovels.

Jesus seized upon this vivid image in one of his more frequent sermons. In it, he would plead with the crowd to "repent" (literally "change your mind") lest they end up in the garbage dump. To a first-century audience, the message was a powerful one. "If you don't turn around and start following God's commands, you will end up throwing your lives away!"

Who can argue with that? Those who live self-centered lives in pursuit of money, power, fame, or sexual gratification miss out on the unequaled joy that comes from honest, loving relationships and lives of service to others. Think about it. How many people have you known who on their deathbeds wished for more money, fame, or sexual conquests? To the contrary, the regrets inevitably concern ruptured relationships, misplaced priorities, and a failure to set worthy goals. Jesus knew that a misspent life was a wasted life, and he wanted to do everything in his power to put people on the path to joyful living.

Now, ending up in life's garbage dump isn't my idea of a nice way to spend eternity, but you got to admit, it's light-years ahead of everlasting torment. The difference is so dramatic, in fact, that I used to carry a picture of the actual Valley of Hinnom around in my Bible to silence my fundamentalist friends when they got all heated up about hell. These days Gehenna is rather pastoral in appearance, with a lot of grass and a few boulders scattered around for the picnickers. When my friends started snorting about the fire and brimstone, I would whip out my picture and say, "Well, I've been to hell. Even got a picture of it. And it looks pretty good to me!" Good, clean fun.

But jokes about Gehenna aside, what should we make of Jesus' parable of Lazarus and the rich man? You remember the story: The rich man winds up in hell and Lazarus, the beggar, ends up in the bosom of Abraham. The rich man's torment is so severe that he begs Lazarus for a drop of water to cool his parched tongue. Doesn't that prove there's a hell?

Probably not. This parable did not originate with Jesus. It was an ancient Egyptian story that Jesus borrowed and then changed to make a critical point. Remember, parables have only *one* point. They are not allegories.

Most first-century Jews believed that money was a sign of God's blessing, just as poverty was a sign of God's curse. (Common theology among televangelists today!) Jesus taught nearly the opposite. Jesus said that God had a special place in his heart for the poor, and special responsibilities for the rich. "To whom much is given, much is required," said Jesus. He went on to suggest that it was nearly impossible for a rich person to find God. "It's easier for a camel to squeeze through the eye of a surgeon's needle," an exasperated Jesus once exclaimed, "than for a rich person to get into heaven!" Jesus used the ancient story of Lazarus and the rich man to make a point about wealth, not about the afterlife. His trick ending, where the poor man is rewarded and the rich man punished, raised the ire of the connected people of his day and moved him one step closer to his appointment with a Roman cross.

There is another reference to hell found in the Gospels. It comes in Jesus' famous statement to Peter, the rough-hewn leader of the disciples: "Henceforth, you shall be called Peter [literally 'rock'], and upon this rock I will build my church, and the gates of hell will not stand against it!" (Matthew 16:18). This is a strong statement, but again, it says nothing about the afterlife. The word used here was "Hades." It's a reference to the ancient underworld, to which all departed souls were thought to descend. According to the Greeks and Romans, it had a massive set of gates from which no soul could escape. Jesus was, again, using a popular image to convey a powerful truth. Nothing—not even Pluto's front door—can hold back the movement we are starting here, Jesus was saying.

The other most common biblical reference to hell is found in the book of Revelation. There John, using highly symbolic language, speaks of the enemies of God being cast into a lake of fire where they are consumed. The Bible calls it the "second death." This is no pleasant consolation to those who refuse God, but it's a far cry from the place of *everlasting* torment preached about in many churches. The biblical fire may be eternal, but the suffering is not.

The bottom line is that there is scant scriptural support for the doctrine of eternal damnation—at least as most Christians understand it. True, the Bible teaches judgment. We all reap what we sow. And death to the nonbeliever means eternal separation from God—which is hell enough, if you ask me. But everlasting torment? The best evidence suggests that this is a human invention designed to scare and manipulate ordinary folk into doing what the church wanted them to do. On the church's worst days, the doctrine of hell was used to extort money. Lots of it. On its

best days, hell was used to encourage lives of moral recti-
tude. Certainly, the church wants to encourage morality
and purposeful living. But scaring people to death is not the
way to do it. Fear wears off, and the church member who is
motivated by it is likely to slip away as the years roll by. But
love never dies. Show people they are loved by God and by
the members of their congregation, and you've won converts for life.

The truth is that no earthly father I've ever known
would torture his child for five seconds, much less an eternity. Neither would the God of the Bible. On the contrary,
everything Jesus taught us about God is undermined by the
notion of hell. Jesus taught that God is love. If our definition of love has degenerated to the point that it allows for
torture, perhaps Charles Manson should be considered as
our next saint.

· 10 ·

How Will It All End?

The end of time ...

Whether it's Stephen Hawking talking about the universe being sucked into a black hole or Pat Robertson promising the imminent return of Christ, the subject fascinates us. Ever since humanity crawled out of the primeval ooze, we've been wondering how it all began. And how it all will end. Even science, with its advances in understanding how life came to be, has been unable to quench our thirst for knowledge about life's final chapter. Will it be a bang or a fizzle? Fire or ice? Several evangelical writers have made fortunes forecasting what no one thus far has been able to forecast. But, twenty-first-century Americans are not alone. Ever since John wrote his dramatic portrayal of the events leading up to the end of time in the book of Revelation, Christians have thought he was talking about them.

The Apostle Paul certainly did. He stressed the point in several of his letters. So did Saint Augustine in the fifth century, Martin Luther in the sixteenth, the Adventists in the nineteenth, and Billy Graham in the twentieth. You won't be surprised to learn that virtually every generation of Christians, especially those facing persecution, concludes that it's living in the "last days" that are referred to in the Bible.

We really can't blame them. Jesus himself seems to have believed that the end of time was imminent. In the twenty-fourth chapter of Matthew, Jesus answers two questions. The first concerns the destruction of the second Jewish temple, which occurred at the hands of the Roman Emperor Titus in A.D. 70. The second concerns the signs of his second coming and the end of time. In Matthew 24:34, Jesus drops the bombshell: "Truly, I say to you, this generation will not pass away until all these things take place!"

The fact that Jesus was mistaken should do nothing to diminish his moral authority, and indeed it hasn't. On the contrary, it serves as a sterling rebuttal of the earliest Christian heresy—namely, the view that Jesus wasn't really human. Humans are fallible. Jesus was fallible. Therefore, Jesus was a human.

For those who consider such sentiments to be heresy, remember Luke's own account of the young carpenter's journey into adulthood: "And Jesus *grew* in wisdom and in stature and in favor with God and man" (Luke 2:52). If Jesus knew everything, he wouldn't need to grow.

Among Christians, there are three major schools of interpretation about the end of time. We'll start with the one most popular among today's evangelicals, and the one behind best-selling books such as the *Late, Great Planet Earth* and the *Left Behind* series. It's called premillennialism. Premillennialists believe that Jesus is going to return to earth one day in bodily form and rule over an earthly kingdom for a thousand years. Before any of that can take place, however, the inhabitants of earth must suffer through a seven-year period of pestilence, destruction, and death. The culmination of this "tribulation" will be the Battle of Armageddon, in which the forces of Satan and his antichrist are defeated by Jesus and a host of angels.

True believers won't have to worry about all this, since they will be transported directly to heaven in an event known as the rapture. Christians will be sucked out of their cars, beds, and golf carts in history's most bizarre aerial display as millions of believers wing their way to the celestial city.

At the conclusion of Christ's thousand-year reign, the forces of evil will again be loosed for a final confrontation with the forces of God. God will win (you could have guessed this), and the bad guys are cast into a lake of fire. The faithful will then be welcomed into the new Jerusalem to be with God forever.

Premillennialsim is based upon a very literal reading of two highly symbolic books of the Bible—Daniel and Revelation, plus a couple of sentences found in Paul's letters to the churches in Corinth and Thessalonica. These Pauline references discuss what will happen to those who are alive at the time of the second coming of Christ, but neither passage supports the notion that believers will be divinely transported out of harm's way before the great tribulation. On the contrary, everything in Christ's teachings suggests that the presence of Christians (who are called to be selfless servants) would be more important than ever during this period of sickness, war, and death. It's hard to imagine that God would withdraw his "best troops" before history's greatest spiritual battle. Remember, Jesus told his followers that they must relinquish their selfish desires, "take up their crosses daily," and follow him. This hardly sounds like the sort of cushy job that would get you out of earth's biggest crisis.

Premillennialism's biggest problem is its literalistic interpretation of books that were never intended to be taken literally. Both Daniel and Revelation are apocalyptic books. Such books were written during periods of intense religious persecution. In order to evade the persecuting authorities, apocalyptic authors adopted symbols and coded language. The goal was to convey messages that were accessible to those inside the religious community but nonsensical to those on the outside.

The book of Revelation fills the bill for symbolic language. Rome, for example, masquerades as ancient Babylon. The emperors become a seven-headed beast. Jerusalem becomes Sodom. Even Jesus is transformed into a lamb.

The book of Daniel is the same way. A massive iron, clay, brass, silver, and gold statue represents successive world empires from Babylon to Greece. The stone that destroys the statue (set in motion "not by human hands") represents, of course, God's special messenger. Using coded language, the book goes on to describe in precise detail the events leading up to the Jewish revolt against the Greeks and Syrians during the second century BC. Even the "abomination of desolation" that is spoken of in Daniel 11 corresponds with the Greek ruler Antiochus Epiphanes' foray into the Jewish temple's inner sanctum (the "Holy of Holies") where he sacrificed a *pig* upon the altar of God and made the priests eat ham sandwiches. Seriously.

Numbers are especially important in apocalyptic writing, for they take on added symbolic meaning. The number seven, for example, represents the divine. Six, one shy of divinity (remember that in Christian lore, Satan was a rebellious angel cast out of heaven), is evil. A trinity of sixes is the epitome of evil, and thus becomes the symbol of the Antichrist. Twelve, representing the twelve tribes of Israel, represents completeness. Twelve squared, therefore, is perfect completeness and is chosen as the number of saints that will be in heaven.

You get the picture. The point is that both Daniel and Revelation are *highly* symbolic. Yet premillennialists insist on taking them literally. Their interpretive faux pas is complicated by the fact that they apply their literalistic approach selectively. They view Christ's perfect reign on earth (ten is the perfect number, so ten times ten becomes the ultimate in perfection) as a literal one thousand years, yet they consider the 144,000 saints in heaven to be symbolic of the complete family of God, which most of them number in the millions. (Jehovah's Witnesses, on the other hand, take the number 144,000 literally.) Premillennialists foresee a literal battle on the plain of Megiddo (i.e., Armageddon), yet none believes that Jesus is returning for that battle with a literal sword sticking out of his mouth, despite this vivid depiction by the author of Revelation. In short, they read Revelation like they read much of the rest of the Bible—claiming to take it all literally, but "spiritualizing" any hard sayings that get in the way, such as Jesus' declaration in Luke 14:33 that "no one can become my disciple who does not give up all of his possessions." Well, not really *all*, they say—just the ones getting between you and God. Read *none*.

Truthfully, no one should entrust their interpretation of Revelation to people without some poetry in their souls.

This blazing story of the forces of good triumphing over the forces of evil can only be understood in light of the fantastic poetic image that it is.

The postmillennialists are like the premillennialists in some ways, but are dramatically different in others. These folks believe in a literal millennium, but they believe Jesus will return *after* it, not before. In short, Christians usher in the kingdom of God through their good works. The Puritans and many in the social gospel movement at the turn of the twentieth century were postmillennialists. Not surprisingly, there aren't many of these folks around today. World War I brought an abrupt end to the naive notion that humanity's good works could bring on such a utopian age. Follow it up with the Great Depression and an even larger world war in which nuclear weapons were introduced, and you can see why we don't have a whole lot of postmillennialists today.

The third major school of interpretation is called amillennialism (literally, "no millennium"). Amillennialists view Revelation and the millennial reign of Christ as largely symbolic—written for a specific audience (namely, the seven churches of Asia Minor) with a specific problem (their persecution by the emperor Domitian). In fact, amillennialism remains the official theory of the Catholic Church. It was this interpretation that brought John's Revelation into the New Testament canon in the first place.

Were it not for the amillennialists, most of us wouldn't even know about the book of Revelation.

The strengths of the amillennial view are considerable. First, it takes history seriously. The books of the Bible were written within a historical context. Take them out of that context, and the books make no sense. The story of Abraham's near sacrifice of his son Issac, for example, makes sense only within a culture that placed great value on child sacrifice.

By viewing Revelation in its historical context, all sorts of things begin to make sense. The seven-headed beast— one with the wound that appeared mortal but was healed—is a symbol for the Roman emperors, from Tiberius (who ruled when Jesus was born) to Domitian (who was rumored to have died but lived, some said, as the reincarnation of Nero). The "mark of the beast"—a necessary mark for anyone wishing to buy or sell—was in fact instituted by Domitian in some parts of Asia Minor as a means of ferreting out all the disloyal subjects who refused to acknowledge the emperor's divinity. These "atheists" were left to forage for themselves outside the bounds of ordinary commerce. Early Christians were persecuted for the "atheism" that was their steadfast refusal to worship the emperor. The biggest clue of all that the amillennialists are on the right track is their explanation of the mysterious number 666. Unlike English and most modern languages,

Greek and Hebrew letters have numerical equivalents. Thus, the number of the beast would be the sum of the separate letters of his name. Six six six happens to be the numerical equivalent of Neron Caesar, the formal Greek spelling for the bloodthirsty emperor who provided the lighting for his garden parties by dipping Christians in oil, placing them atop poles, and lighting them. The certainty of the amillennial interpretation is clinched when you consider the number of ancient manuscripts that substitute the number 616 for 666. The former is the numerical equivalent of Nero Caesar, the more popular name of the above-mentioned leader and the one by which we know him today.

Second, the amillennial view is the one most consistent with the statements of Jesus, Peter, and Paul—namely, that no one—not even the angels in heaven—know when the end of the world will come. Rather, say these three, it will come like "a thief in the night." Christians will do well to remember this the next time a preacher gets out his time lines and charts.

I will take the liberty of adding a fourth school of interpretation—panmillennialism. I can't recall where I first encountered it, but the essence of it is this: Trust God, and in the end things will all pan out.

Now that's good theology.

◆

So What?

✦

As the inhabitants of a single speck of dirt hurtling through space at sixty thousand miles per hour around a nameless star that is one among billions of stars in a galaxy that is also one among billions, we humans get it. We're not in charge.

Life is a mystery. So powerful and unfathomable is the force behind it that we bow before it and give it a name: God. Sometimes it is so palpable that we are left speechless. Like the way we felt when we watched our firstborn child draw her first breath. At other times, it is faint—like the footsteps of a kitten or shadows on a cloudy day. But even then, we sense it. It hums beneath the everyday busyness of our lives.

At its best, religion reminds us that life has meaning and purpose beyond our limited capacity to understand and that we do well to approach the mystery with the humility that comes from being among the "created" rather than the creator.

But there is a danger let loose in the world—a danger that is the height of human hubris clothed in the unseemly garb of false modesty. It is the claim to know the unknowable, namely, the mind of God in all its fullness, and being so cocksure about it that we impose our views upon everyone else.

At gunpoint.

It is four young men flying a jumbo jet into an office tower filled with innocent people. But it is also a cabal of Baptist preachers announcing to the nation that God has decreed that all true believers should abandon the public schools.

Christianity, like Islam, is in danger of being hijacked by a militant minority of fundamentalists. Though less violent than their Muslim counterparts, these fundamentalist Christians are altering the very essence of the faith. Where Jesus preached mercy, they preach judgment. Where Jesus welcomed women, they subordinate them. Where Jesus said to turn the other cheek, they get out their deer rifles. And where Jesus made clear that *all* nations stand under the judgment of God, they have made God the national mascot.

This book has tried to make the case that Christianity

need not be sexist, homophobic, militaristic, or materialistic to be authentic. On the contrary, biblical Christianity, as it was practiced in the early churches, was none of these things.

It is my sincere prayer that two millennia after the death of its founder, Christianity can recapture its vision of creating a world where love of one's neighbor—be she Christian or Muslim, gay or straight, Republican or Democrat—reigns supreme.